sundance
publishing

LITTLE RED
READERS

Little and Big

PETER SLOAN &
SHERYL SLOAN

A stamp is little.

A newspaper is big.

A mouse is little.

A hippopotamus is big.

A toy box is little.

A house is big.

A kitten is little.

A cat is big.

A toothpick is little.

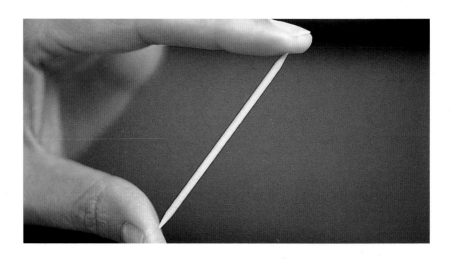

A telephone pole is big.

An ant is little.

An anteater
is big.

A baby is little.

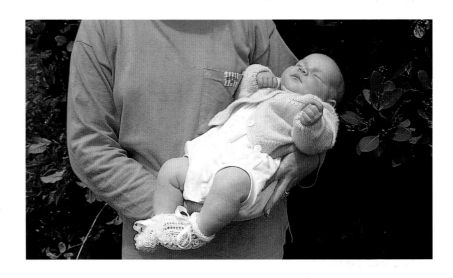

I am big.